One Stands Guard,

One Sleeps
Nancy Scott

Plain View Press
P. O. 42255
Austin, TX 78704

plainviewpress.net
sb@plainviewpress.net
512-441-2452

Copyright Nancy Scott 2009. All rights reserved.
ISBN: 978-1-891386-32-9
Library of Congress Number: 2009924865

Acknowledgements

Thanks to the following publications in which these poems first appeared:

"Breaker Boys" and "Dialogue in Black and White" in *Out of Line*; "Death Attends a Poetry Reading" in *Mad Poets Review*; "Faculty Wives, circa 1968" in *Kelsey Review*; "Hampstead Again" in *Delaware Valley Poets Anthology*; "How Burma Shave Saved the Day," "Paradise," and "The Sleeping Gypsy" in *U.S.1 Worksheets*; "A Kid Called Diamond" in *Struggle*; "Leah at Two: Octoberfest" and "Nine years old, Rickey can't read" in *Slant, A Journal of Poetry*; "Life Cycle of Argument" in *New York Quarterly*; "Mama's Closet" in *The Journal of New Jersey Poets*; "Maria, Curacao, Christmas 1957" in *The Bucks County Writer*; "On the El, Chicago" and "Saturday night alone, I surf the Net" in *Schuylkill Valley Journal*; "Princeton: The Alchemist & Barrister, 1990" in *Poet Lore*; "Red Skelton on the Ponte Vecchio" in *Exit 13*; "Safe Place at Wilder Park" in *The Carriage House Poetry Series, Tenth Anniversary Anthology*; "Seven-year-old boy found dead in plastic storage bin" in *J Journal*; "William" in *Big Scream*.

Cover art by Robert V.P. Davis. Front Cover: "Tree in the Pink", Back Cover: "The Old Country."

Cover design by Susan Bright.

Contents

The Sleeping Gypsy   7

Part I: Burma Shave

Poet at Seven   11
How Burma Shave Saved the Day   13
Nine Years Old, Rickey Can't Read   14
Mannheim Road   15
How My Brother Got Religion   16
My Life as an Artist   18
The Louse, or How I Got a Brother, or Didn't   19
Cars   21
The Park Sheraton Hotel, New York City   22
On the El, Chicago   23
Family Chronicles   24
Bonds for Israel   26
Playing Chess with the Muskrat   28
The Cost of Things   29
The Pasta Maker   30
High School Graduation Photo   31
Of Winter and Wings, 2007   32
Leah on Politics   33
Leah on Shopping   34
Leah at Octoberfest   35
Leaving Montreal with My Son   36

Part II: Dining with Death

The Boy with Ice Eyes   39
Paradise   40
Mixed Greens   42
Death Attends a Poetry Reading   43
Breaker Boys   44
A Kid Called Diamond   45
Seven-Year-Old Boy Found Dead in Plastic Storage Bin, 2003   46
Paul and Cheryl   47
Pink Fluffy Slippers   48
Mama's Closet   49
Lyla, 1992   50

Ballerina	51
Maria, Curacao, 1957	52
William	53
The Patriarch's Wall	55

Part III: Across Time

Sweet Fourteen, USO, Miami Beach, 1952	59
Passing Through Northern New Jersey in Late August, 1959	61
Paradise Italian Style	63
Faculty Wives, Circa 1968	65
Snapshot of an Ivy League Faculty Wife	67
Counting Backwards in London	68
Life Cycle of Argument	69
Across Time	70
Negotiating	72
The Clock Repairer	73
At The Alchemist & Barrister, Princeton, New Jersey	74
Dialogue in Black and White	75
Hampstead Again	76
Noodle Doctor	77
Teterboro Airport	78
Antigua	79
Red Skelton on the Ponte Vecchio	80
Revelation	81
Saturday Night Alone, I Surf the Net	82
Safe Place at Wilder Park	83

About the Author	85
About the Artist	86

*What does God see through the window
while his hands reach into the world?*

– Yehudi Amichai

The Sleeping Gypsy

after Henri Rousseau

The melody of the lute lured the big cat. Fearless, the gypsy
offered him water from her cupped hands. Then, she bid the lion

stay, sang of unrequited love, hardship, the gypsy's lot, how she'd
roamed thick forest, searing desert, cast out from *kumpania*, family.

At dusk, she read the lion's paw and lied to him, as she does to all
not of her kind, whispered, if he stayed by her, she knew a way

from these barren dunes to a great savanna filled with creatures
to sate his appetite. He could kill a fatty ewe, she'd roast it, together

they would eat it to their liking. No misgivings about taking beast
as companion. *Lion,* she said, *we'll travel like the water.* No foot-

prints, no dream of home, just life along the *lungo drom,* long road.
So it is with survival: one stands guard, one sleeps.

Part 1
Burma Shave

Poet at Seven

1.

I was an only child.
We were Jewish.
We didn't believe in Jesus Christ
or Heaven.
We didn't celebrate Christmas,
except that year we did.

On a small table, an electric
tree with bubbling colored lights.
A gift to Christine, our live-in,
because she went to Church.
Christine taught me the words
to *We Three Kings* and *Silent Night*.

2.

My parents were going to die.
They flew everywhere
in those crazy Constellations
that were always crashing.
I had nightmares
I'd end up in the orphanage
out on Wolf Road.
It was run by nuns.
I'd heard they were mean to the kids.

Christine taught me how to make
perfect square corners on my bed.
Knowing how to do this
might help me fit in.

continued...

3.

My parents didn't die.
In August of my seventh year,
they adopted a baby boy.
They called him Richard
after my father.

My father was happy, he had a son.
Christine was happy, she loved babies.
My mother was happy, she could go
back to work. She had Christine.

I felt like an orphan again.

4.

I started second grade
at Poplar Elementary.
All the elementary schools
were named after trees – Hawthorne,
Mulberry, Pine.
Peter was in third grade.
He fell through the ice and almost drowned.
We became friends.

There's more, Reader, but it came
much later.
Peter and I grew up together.
Everyone expected us to get married.
We did, but to other people.
Peter died in a car crash.
My husband refused to let me
name any of our sons *Peter*.

How Burma Shave Saved the Day

Sunday afternoon, road out of Sycamore.
"A short-cut," Dad says, just miles of blacktop

dissecting cornfields, saucer-eyed cows giving us
the once-over. Rickey and I locked in the back seat

for hours, straight from a boring visit with
Uncle Seymour who sells cheap print dresses

and smells of cigars. Our fingers draw pouty mouths,
flying ringlets, tic-tac-toe grids on the frosty windows.

"Stop that." Mom whips her arm from the front seat
and misses. Rickey grabs his throat. "I'm gonna

throw up if we don't stop soon." Then we spot them,
the signs at the side of the road:

*Cattle Crossing / Means Go Slow / That Old Bull /
Is Some Cow's Beau / Burma Shave*

Suddenly we're on an adventure, one set of signs
means another ahead. Sure enough, but in the opposite

direction. We crane our necks.

*Burma Shave / I'll Cook The Rice / The Wedding's Off /
And Said, No Dice / She Eyed His Beard*

We can't be stopped. *Pat's bristles*–bouncing–*Scratched*
–faster and faster–*Bridget's nose*–giggling–*That's when*
–ducking–*Her wild Irish rose*–until *Burma Shave* hours

become whispers and it's dark when we get home.

Nine Years Old, Rickey Can't Read

Twice a week, Miss Dawson, retired-blue-haired spinster,
tried to teach my brother phonics.
She needed the money. She'd wag an arthritic finger,
cackle *stubborn boy bad apple*.
It was a hellish hour.

Rickey coveted Hopalong Cassidy's pearl-handled pistols
but snatched Miss D's eighteenth-century mantel clock
and brandished it like a weapon.
Miss D treasured that old clock. She grabbed for it,
he held tight, lurched backwards.
The clock whacked Rickey's front teeth in half.

It was 1954. Mom and Dad didn't take my brother
to a dentist, but a pricey shrink
who declared Rickey's refusal to read the result
of deep-seated repression
over his adoption (six-day-old infant) and their insecurities.
Rickey lassoed childhood in a Stetson, blasted our parents
away with dream pistols, smirked
his imperfect mouth, and never passed a reading test.

Aboard the USS Ranger stranded in the Gulf of Tonkin
in 1966, Rickey won his GED playing poker.
Later, he made millions in construction, hired people
to read for him.
At 60, he wears his broken teeth like a merit badge,
hates our dead parents, says he wishes
he'd smashed the crap out of that stupid clock.

Mannheim Road

Dad liked to speed on Mannheim Road.
Every cop knew our license plates.
Pulled over, Dad would slip two fins

into the ready glove. *For the missus
and kids,* he'd say, smiling,
then we'd be on our way.

That day, my brother was in the front seat
puking out the window.
I, at twelve, slouched in the back

and worried about
the disposition of our souls.
It's wrong to bribe a cop, I whined.

I'm doing this for you, Dad said, foot
heavy again. *Next week, the train.*
Rickey turned and growled at me.

I buried my head in an Archie comic.
Each trip to visit Grandma Becky
routed us closer to Hell.

How My Brother Got Religion

It wasn't me, I'm quick to protest
when Mother catches us
admiring Rickey's loot: power drill,

hacksaw, claw hammer, pliers,
filched from *St. Somebody's Church
on Oak Street,* Rickey blurts.

Nippy October night deepening,
the two of us trudge a mile
to the church, lugging tools

in a canvas bag, a mighty gust
blowing dead leaves in our faces.
Scowl darker than Mother's,

Rickey says, *I should've taken
the whole toolbox. Made it
worthwhile if I didn't get caught.*

That's stupid, I say, burrowing my chin
in my woolen scarf. *Remember
the priest can have you arrested.*

Rickey shuffles to the great oak door
and knocks. I crouch
in the bushes, mittens covering

my ears, shutting out the pipe organ's
unearthly groaning.
I'm stiff as a statue when Rickey

reappears, empty-handed.
What did the priest say?
Rickey hurls rocks at an unlucky pigeon.

*He didn't say anything, but I hope
he drowns in his holy water.*

My Life as an Artist

When I was eight,
I spent Saturday mornings at Mrs. Hoy's
leafing through books and magazines
for a picture to copy – bird, Dutch boy skating,
sailboat, red barn and silo.
Your daughter is gifted, Mrs. Hoy would say
as my mother wrote another tuition check.

Standing at my easel, Mrs. Hoy was less kind.

If you tried harder, you could do this.
With swift brush, she'd paint my watercolor
to her liking, then insist I sign my name in the corner.
To please my mother, I continued this charade
until staring at the perfect scarlet tanager hanging
in our hall, my mother thought to say,
Why don't you ever draw this well at home?

So ended my life as a watercolorist.

The following winter, my mother hired Fred.
He taught a class in oils around a pot-bellied stove
in the cluttered space above his garage.
Frantic, I painted still life – orange pear cup bowl –
convinced hot coals and fumes would set the place
on fire. *Your daughter has a real passion for art,*
Fred told my mother.

I begged her to let me take piano lessons.

The Louse, or How I Got a Brother, or Didn't

In the '40s, we all knew Cousin Bernie
as a louse, despite a likeness to Erroll Flynn.

Fed up with shoehorning pumps two sizes
too small onto local matrons' fat feet, Bernie

wheedled into Aunt Clara's affections.
Childless, she thrived on the attention, handed

over her trust fund, which Bernie looted
and lost on the ponies. Aunt Clara died

of a broken heart. We slogged through mud
on our way to the gravesite, Bernie's wailing

the loudest. When rumors spread – two thugs
asking around – Bernie hightailed it

out of town. Last we heard of him? Not quite.
Dad was always helping stray relatives, bailed

them out of foreclosures, paid to have their kids' teeth
straightened, or, like Bernie in *Shoes*, gave them jobs

in the family business. Bernie got the hots for Peg
in *Better Dresses*. With flaming hair, a perfect figure

draped in green crepe, Marine hubby dead in some
forsaken jungle in the Pacific, Peg was overripe

for Bernie's charms. Our swashbuckling cousin
knocked her up, left her with swollen ankles and belly,

continued...

and later, a colicky baby that wouldn't shut up.
Kid's a spitting image of the louse, Peg said, as she

helped herself to the cash receipts. Dad fired her,
but didn't press charges. *Not even a postcard*, she groused,

and put the little howler up for adoption. That's how
I got my brother. Or, there's no truth to any of this,

except the part where Daddy has a soft heart.

Cars

My father restored antique cars: '03 Model A Ford,
'07 Orient Buckboard, '17 Stutz Bearcat, '24 Model T,

'25 Dodge; and a classic, '37 Cord, like the one
Tom Mix crashed and died in, in Arizona. Much

speculation if gears slipping or vapor locks could be
blamed for the accident, so Dad made me promise

to ease up on the gas, but the Cord was sporty, sleek
leather interior, hooded lights, tough to hold back.

My first convertible, yellow Dodge with rumble seat.
The Buckboard so primitive, Dad disassembled

and rebuilt it on our ping-pong table. Others arrived
hopeless on flat beds of trucks, took off months later,

spiffed up and purring. Except the '36 Cord cannibalized
for parts until it looked like a Thanksgiving carcass.

On meet days, Dad donned a long white duster and cap,
cranked his shiny roadster, waved good-bye, and off

they went, no regard for the latest grass widow, elegant
new Fleetwood, with V-8 engine, whitewalls, and fins.

The Park Sheraton Hotel, New York City

Albert Anastasio, Cosa Nostra boss,
was gunned down in a barber's chair
at the Park Sheraton fifteen months before
my father dropped dead on the sidewalk
in front of the same barber shop.

Reports say at 7:46 that morning,
Dad, who was wearing a striped bathrobe
over his pajamas, no wallet, just change
from the newspaper, was headed toward
the revolving door. They say no one

could identify him until an attractive
red-head staying at the hotel came
to the front desk and asked if anyone
had seen a bald man in striped bathrobe.
By then, he'd been taken by ambulance

to the hospital, then to the morgue.
Cause of death, coronary occlusion.
Then the arrangements: shipping the body
home to Chicago, the funeral, the flowers,
the timely burial, according to custom.

My mother reclaiming the man who, years
earlier, had left her for the red-haired whore
– same woman who badgered the clerk
to remember if he'd seen a forty-eight-year-old
man in striped robe carrying *The New York Times*,

which later referred to my father as
"an unidentified male", but had titillated
America for months with details
of the life and demise of a notorious killer.

On the El, Chicago

Old woman, felt hat stuck with a pheasant feather,
you sit down across the aisle, fumble
with the broken clasp of your purse.

Something familiar in the way shadow
highlights pale fuzz of your cheek.
The decades haven't changed you

much – same sturdy shoes, lisle stockings
rolled to the knee with elastic bands,
rimless glasses, shapeless coat disguising

the slow curve of spine. I can smell brisket
and kugel Sunday dinners, taste cookies,
rock hard, straight from the oven.

For Jackie's mutt, you'd wrap a knucklebone,
but joke I'd never find a husband.
Truth, old woman, I've never wanted

for men. To keep me from the conversation,
you spoke Yiddish. If not words,
I understood intent – chiding Dad

for buying you a wool coat, a ticket
to visit other grandkids. For him
this was the measure of a man.

The El lurches into Montrose station.
You rise and exit like you always did
when you didn't want to hear.

Family Chronicles

Truth is, Stuart and I are not related,
though not from lack of trying.
He calls the other day to catch me up

on Cousin Harvey, who died, a day short
of ninety, in Chicago. *Huge write-up
in newspapers*, Stuart says.

He was a big-shot philatelist.
Harvey's my cousin so I say,
How do you know him?

He and my mother went to the same synagogue,
Stuart says. *Ever hear of Sycamore,
southwest of Chicago?*

I tell him I've written a poem about
Uncle Seymour who owns a dress shop there.
I'd love to read it, Stuart says, *but his name*

was Louie. He died last month.
Was he yours or mine? I ask.
Mine, Stuart says.

As we tally names, mostly deaths now,
and divvy up relatives, Stuart reminds me
our grandmothers were best friends

in the early 1900s. Pity, the marriage between
Mother and Stuart's uncle Marvin never happened.
Later, my parents tried to marry me off

to Stuart's cousin Philip.
In the '70s, both widowed, Mother and Marvin
eyed each other and blinked.

In the '90s, Philip and I, both divorced, failed
chemistry again.
Today Stuart and I, thicker than blood, soldier on.

Bonds for Israel

When my brother Richard and I opened our mother's
safe deposit box in 1985, we found among her papers

one State of Israel bond, long past due.
In the early '50s, buying bonds was a hot topic

in our family. My parents argued about whether to
support a Jewish state, Dad insisting we should,

Mother equally opposed. I didn't understand the issues,
but I sided with my father because I liked him better.

At my relatives' tables, I'd watch an irate aunt or uncle
fling down a napkin on a plate of kugel and storm out

the back door. For a moment, stone silence, as if everyone
were busy saying a prayer for the departed, except

my grandmother, who, hard of hearing, shouted,
"What's happened this time?"

My beloved Aunt Sylvia took me aside, whispered,
"Your mother's not a good Jew." What did she mean?

We didn't keep kosher or go to temple except on
High Holy Days? She didn't either.

Could it have something to do with Mother's refusal
to recognize Israel? I sensed she only used this

as an excuse to fight with Dad.
Besides, Mother taught our cook how to make

all the right dishes for special occasions. Plastic covers
came off when relatives flocked to the house,

and my brother and I were immaculate trophy children.
After Mother had a stroke, she took pleasure in

informing Richard and me that only one of us
would inherit her fortune. We'd decided long before

we cremated her that we'd split everything fifty-fifty.
The lone State of Israel bond landed in my pile, along with

worthless stock in the Singer Sewing Machine Company,
which went broke after its patent ran out.

What to do with the bond?
I knew the others had been cashed. I could redeem it

or frame it. Didn't need the two-fifty plus interest.
But why had Mother kept it? An oversight?

Probably not. A souvenir from the argument she'd lost?
Or proof she was a believer? I doubt it.

Playing Chess with the Muskrat

It's three a.m. I can't sleep. I'm playing chess
with the Muskrat. He's beating me.
"Hey, kiddo," I say, "I know you moved
the bishop when you thought I wasn't looking."
"Hey, insomniac, you got someone else
to keep you company?"
"Careful, Muskrat. I remember the jacket
my mother had made out of your kin."
"Yeah, yeah," the Muskrat says. "Let's play."

I think of all those furs I coveted as a kid.
My mother's foxes – hard, beady eyes, sharp
nails – draped around her neck. Nobody messed
with my mother with, or without, the foxes.
I don't mention her silky Russian sable,
the chinchilla, three-quarter curly Persian lamb
and matching hat, or full-length mink
I had remodeled so it fits me now.

"Ah, Muskrat, life's too short. Checkmate."

The Cost of Things

Hot August afternoon, we're on our way
to Ugolino, fancy country club closed to locals,
on the outskirts of Firenze. We enter a small shop

on a back street near the Arno. Inside, the air is
thick and musty. Multi-colored plastic strips dangle
in the doorway. Dust coats everything.

The shopkeeper eyes us suspiciously. Only crazy
tourists visit Firenze the month Italians flee.
We need a float for Mikey, who can't swim.

A red, white. and green plastic ring, fully inflated,
hangs above assorted cooking pans.
Quanto costa? I ask. The shopkeeper rattles off a price

in lire, sixteen dollars. I shake my head.
Mikey finds a red pail and shovel, tries to free them
from a web of plastic yellow netting.

Not that, I say, pulling the netting from his grasp.
There's no sand at Ugolino.
The shopkeeper glares, runs a hand through his unruly

mane. Unhooks the plastic ring and offers it
to Mikey. *Let's go,* I say. *It costs too much.*
Mikey's tear-stained face turns crimson. *No. I want*

that thing. Stamps his feet, raising dust huge as horse flies.
I want to drown in the cool water at Ugolino.
I offer the shopkeeper a fistful of lire. He takes the money,

pulls the plug, and squashes out hissing air. Thrusts
the flattened ring at me. *Ciao,* he snorts, as I yank my son
toward the door and Mikey lets out another howl.

The Pasta Maker

When Jimmy was twelve, he gave up the idea of raising
miniature horses – our yard a half-acre shy of city regulation.

His next venture – making homemade pasta. I like to think
the efforts of those agile hands, which cranked out strips

of flour and water, then draped them to dry on any
useful object – towel bars, hangers, railings – fostered

Jimmy's star as a wide-receiver. Billy, two years older,
tough act to follow on the football field, found fresh pasta

dripping from the bars of his headboard, said, *This is crap*,
and would only agree to eat pasta from the supermarket.

The nightly competition began: two boys, two boiling pots –
one with fresh pasta, the other with store brand penne,

rigatoni, or linguine. Somehow they sorted out whose turn
to brown the meat and onions. Jimmy created prime-time

sauce and insisted on grating blocks of aged Romano.
To have kids who'll do the cooking, what a bonus!

Now Jimmy rustles up on moment's notice, sautéed orange
roughy, talapia with fresh lime salsa, vegetable ragouts.

Homemade pasta? *Too many carbs*, he says. Shiny pasta-
maker, boxed and labeled, dusty relic on the shelf.

High School Graduation Photo

for Jimmy

Fake desert orange sunset, the photo
making him a thirty-something man, face
fleshed-out, dark suit and tie, slightly receding
hairline, not the lean, muscular boy athlete
with curly hair and crafted stance that drove
teenage girls to do wicked things, so at first,
I felt cheated, wanted Jimmy recorded on film
as he really looked the day he graduated,
and all those nights I'd listened for the click
of the lock before I could sleep, late afternoons
outside the gym when he'd toss his backpack
onto the rear seat, grumble, *Wasserman throws
like a girl, we'll never get a berth at the States,*
but somehow the camera had captured my son
in a strange time warp, reassuring me
my fears about Jimmy flipping his dirt bike,
wrapping his car around a tree, random
crossfires were baseless, so even after he said,
Throw it away, it doesn't look like me, I kept it
in the bottom tray of my jewelry box, along with
the first curl I'd snipped when he was a baby,
and years later, when he sent me a snapshot
taken at a San Francisco nightclub, I laid
the two side-by-side, they were so much alike,
his arms loosely crossed at the wrists, high
forehead, pretty girl leaning into his shoulder.

Of Winter and Wings, 2007

By mid-January, the mercury has soared
into the seventies. I dig up dead
winter pansies and release water
into the outdoor spigots.
Inside, I fill the fruit bowl with lemons.
Migrating birds continue to cruise
in disarray. Unable to fix direction,
they've stayed for the winter, a misnomer.
The season has flown the coop.
Where are the hard-pack winters?
Ground covered in snow from November
to March, lake frozen for miles,
the skritch of our skates on the ice,
which reminds me
I need more powdered sugar
to make lemon squares
for my three-year-old granddaughter.
Leah and I track around the pond
where we discover a whole fallen wing.
She stoops and peers at the wing
and refuses to leave.
How does the bird fly? she asks.
I say, *Maybe it will grow a new wing.*
In this bizarre season, who can say
otherwise?

Leah on Politics

Obama is too churchy, Leah says.
What does "churchy" mean? I ask.
I don't know, she says, shrugging
her shoulders.

Leah does understand politics
closer to home – *I love you, Mimi.*
I love you, too, I say, wondering
what this is going to cost me –
ice cream, another stuffed cow,
a visit to the farm to pet Coco the lamb?

I don't have a brother or sister,
Leah says. *Can I get a hamster?*
The pet store crosses my mind, briefly.
I heed my own words: you buy it, you own it.
I've cared for all the pets I intend to – six dogs,
several cats, dozens of fish, and a bird.

You'll have to convince Mommy and Daddy.
My refusal drains Leah's patience.
I hate you, she says.
*You're not always my favorite buttercup
either*, I say, giving her a bear hug,
which she wiggles out of.

In a minute we'll be best friends
and take our tree branch walking sticks
out on the path again.

Leah on Shopping

Animal Crackers have gone the way of Farina.
Leah wouldn't be caught dead carrying

the little red and yellow box with its string handle.
Forget Farina. I tell her when I was a kid, I ate it

laced with brown sugar and butter. She rolls her eyes
at my dinosaur tale. I avoid stores that offer

pint-sized shopping carts, with pint-sized flags
and signs: *Future Shopper*. Leah doesn't need

inducements. Today a lanky old man guards
samples of Special K's new cinnamon and pecan.

Leah wolfs a miniature cupful. *More*, she says.
The man hands her a coupon. She thrusts it at me,

grabs a full cup with each hand and darts away.
Clutching a super-sized cereal box, I say,

Let's go to the park. You can climb on the monkey bars.
Leah says, *Let's go to the mall and buy a pink bear.*

But you have a million stuffed animals.
Arms akimbo, she slits her eyes and stamps her left

Nike sneaker. *I need to rescue another one
from the shelf.* She tugs on my hand. I'm captured.

Leah at Octoberfest

Elmo and Sponge Bob were there
and a fairy princess in pink and white net,
Spiderman and clowns,
and pumpkins too,
and scarecrows in chewed-up felt hats.

But Leah, with a hot dog in her left hand,
a jug of blue juice in her right, couldn't take
her eyes off the monster
she didn't have a name for yet: Grim Reaper
– hooked nose, red eyes, black cloak,
bloody cardboard scythe – and two paces
behind him a pint-sized double.

From the pony ride, the plastic bubble
trampoline, the haystacks she kept lookout
for the monster. Then he was in front of her
coming closer. She dug into her pocket
for the handful of stones she'd collected,
was about to fling them in his direction,
when he suddenly squatted
and tied the shoelaces
of his side-kick sitting on a bench.

Look, she shouted, *he's a Daddy*,
and dismissed him as only a child can.

Leaving Montreal with My Son

for Michael

I had trouble sleeping our last night in Montreal.

Darkness rose over stone buildings, cobblestones
                      to the ancient harbor,
encircled the trees, leaves brittled by frost,
      wires strung like fishing nets across the sky.

We'd criss-crossed the old city, bought graphics
      and steaming coffee, strolled corridors
underground where people have no need to venture
      into daylight.

At the Botanical Garden, late October had wizened
      outdoor blooms. Inside the greenhouse, children
clapped and giggled as Esmeralda, the friendly witch,
      prattled on in French.

Reached Atwater Market where pumpkins were stacked high,
      perfect green, yellow, red peppers, leeks, lettuce,
            every kind of berry lined open stalls.
Feast of sausages, rabbit, lamb, goose livers, brioche, cheeses.

Heavy mist followed us to the border,
      quarts of dijon and a carved wooden bird
           with three-foot wing span tucked in our trunk.
A bored customs guard asked us why
      we'd gone to Montreal.

Why would anyone want to leave?

Part II
Dining with Death

The Boy with Ice Eyes

for Jimmy

Death was hungry, needed a fix,
watched the boy with ice eyes
drive a '64 Mustang up Potrero Hill.

Death growled, *It's getting late,*
as the Mustang hovered ready to fly
down the other side of the hill.

The boy's foot hit the gas,
Death lunged, snatched the brake hoses.
The Mustang careened at 55 mph
straight for the traffic on Third.

His ice eyes took aim to make the turn,
hands steady, the boy rammed
the Mustang into the granite wall
of the United Methodist Church.

KABOOM

All Hell broke loose.
Angels on duty that night
took after Death with a Flying Wedge.
Time froze, owls gasped,
the moon scooted behind the church spire.

The boy climbed out
of the demolished car
without a scratch.

Death shook off dirt from Potrero Hill,
looked at the car, looked at the boy,
spat out a feather.

Paradise

A waif-like creature with long dark hair
and piercing eyes walked into
a café on the upper West Side, ordered
double espresso and a bear claw.

"Do you mind?" She slipped into a chair
across from me. "I'm Paradise," she said.
I said, "What an unusual name."
She broke off a chunk of bear claw
and popped it into her mouth. "I'm always hungry.
I think I've got a second stomach."

That afternoon, I ran into Paradise
wolfing a burger, asked her where she was from.
"I'm not sure," she said. "Sometimes
I think I'm from Alabama, but then I get this image
of snow. Maybe I'm from a place that's cold."
She crinkled her nose.

"I'd love to hang out and hear more," I said,
"but I have to pick up my daughter from dance class."
"Your daughter's lucky to have a mom,"
Paradise said. "I must have one somewhere,
but I'm not sure I can find her."

A week went by. I grew impatient
to see Paradise. Imagine my shock –
she'd shaved her head.
"I sold my hair to a wigmaker," she said.
"I needed the money." She pirouetted right there
on the sidewalk. "And, there's more..." She did
a soft shoe shuffle around the telephone pole.
"I've landed the part of a gamine in a snuff film."

Alarmed, I said, "You know how that ends?"
"Don't worry," Paradise said. "It's all done with
mirrors. Isn't everything?"

Mixed Greens

After a spate of relatives dying, funeral wreaths, heels
sticking in mud on the way to the gravesite,
I decided to dine with Death to discuss the situation.
I love what you're wearing, said Death to jump-start
the conversation.
Hand-screened poppies on silk, I said. *Are you partial to red?*
I'm color blind, said Death.
Once, I turned a few heads in this dress.
I remember, Death smiled as he signaled the waiter.
He ordered the juiciest rib on a standing rib roast, grilled root
vegetables, and pricey Bordeaux for himself.
The lady will have mixed greens.
Sensing my displeasure, he explained it like this:
Do you think I'll be free for dinner forever?
No, I said.
Do you sit all day in front of a computer?
Yes, I said.
He slathered butter on a crescent roll.
Never lift a finger to exercise?
True, I said.
And those Big Macs and fries you love so much?
I hung my head.
You'll thank me later, said Death.

Death Attends a Poetry Reading

He sets his shabby book-bag on the floor,
slips into the seat beside me,
pinning me against the wall.
He turns and smiles, his brow
a well-traveled map, thick blunt fingers
splayed across his thighs.
Like an archwind, his sweet breath
whips around the room,
riffles book pages,
rags on the speaker's words,
spilling them in corners,
swirling them like grain.
Inches from my shoulder, he leans
as if to whisper.
Silence, no applause.

Breaker Boys

after Growing Up in Coal Country
by Susan Campbell Bartoletti

Dust, smoke, and steam turn boys, as young as five,
coal-black. They hunch like old men, on pine boards
set across long iron chutes, bear the monotony,

the racket, the whips for a day's twenty-five cents.
Chew tobacco, cover their mouths with cloth
to block the bitter air. Ten, twelve hours, gloveless

fingers snatch debris – slate and rock – from rushing coal.
Fingers swell and bleed. At night, mothers rub in goose
grease to toughen up the tips. After a luckless lad

stumbled down a chute and smothered, his mother went
mad with grief. Tomorrow another might lose his leg,
his fingers. Boys learn how to sabotage conveyers, reap

more time to play ball at noon. Dream of first jobs
underground: nipper, spragger, mule driver. Envy
the older ones' freedom in miles of dark tunnels,

echo-free chambers, absent of supervision; still
mindful of shift and splinter, roof collapse, fire, rats,
ghosts, water trickling deep within Earth's gut.

A Kid Called Diamond

from the files of an Innocence Project

The story goes: a black man pulls a gun in the sub-
shop parking lot and shoots a Latino point blank.

Witnesses agree the shooter was wearing white sneakers
and a dark coat ending well below his knees, although

they disagree who first recognized him by his street name,
Diamond. While this is going down, the seventeen-year-old

is hangin' in Jim & Mary's Bar, strutting his new brown
leather bomber jacket and leather boots. Cops say he did it

for drugs he wasn't known to use, maybe a boost here
and there, no record. Besides, talk on the street makes

his cousin the shooter. No matter. The jury convicts
Diamond of first degree murder, life with no chance of parole.

For fifteen years, Diamond insists he's innocent.
What can he do? Police reports disappeared, prosecutor's

a judge, defense attorney lost his notes. No prints on the gun
turned in by a stranger. The cousin, inside for another murder,

won't talk. Some say Diamond would have killed sooner
or later, people don't end up in prison without good reason.

Seven-Year-Old Boy Found Dead in Plastic Storage Bin, 2003

He slipped through the cracks,
past allegation and ink
smudged in a six-digit number.

Deep tissue bruising, they said.
Blunt instrument, they said.
A terrible mistake, they said.

Come here, child, and give
Mama some sugar.

Paul and Cheryl

Paul had Cheryl's blonde hair and blue eyes.
Ricardo beat her, said the kid wasn't his.
When I saw the bruises
I asked Cheryl why she stayed.
Ricardo's got AIDS, he needs me, she said.

Cheryl brought Paul in when he was two.
She looked pale and edgy. *Ricardo?*
Cheryl shook her head. *He's really sick.*
All he does is yell. His mother's here
but only to collect her cut. She's letting
dealers use Ricardo's brother like a mule.

Lifting the child to her lap, Cheryl said,
I have ovarian cancer. The doctors
give me less than six months.
Paul wriggled around, screwing his face up.
Cheryl jingled a key ring
trying to quiet him. It seemed useless to ask if
she'd pursued all her options. *What will you do?*

Paul started to wail.
I can't leave him with Ricardo's mother.
She held Paul to her chest where he calmed
to a whimper. *My parents don't want him.*
She looked me straight on. *I trust you,*
she said. *Would you take him?*

                    *

The call came three months later, Cheryl
was dead, Paul placed in foster care.

Pink Fluffy Slippers

No, I wasn't raped.
I wanted to do it.
Boys like me. Having sex
makes me feel pretty.
Promise you won't tell
my mom, she'd kill me.

I remember this photo.
It's a slumber party
when I was eight,
me and Rachel wearing
Barbie nightgowns
and pink fluffy slippers.

Sometimes the boys say
they love me.
They buy me things,
like CDs or stuffed bears.
Joey, he gave me
cool blue and white sneakers.
Sometimes lots of boys do it.
It doesn't hurt so much.

I wish you'd leave me alone.
No one, not even you,
is going to stop me.

Mama's Closet

Be quiet, Mama says, before she turns the key.
In the morning we'll do something special.
Don't want him to think I've got a child.

He fears what comes in at night. Imagines
the stranger's body wrapped around his mama.
Hears the groaning and thinks the man must be
hurting her. He whimpers but there's nothing
he can do locked in Mama's closet.

From his dark outpost, he tries to peek
through the strip of light beneath the door,
but can't see anything. Like an odd shoe
among tossed pairs, he rubs his hand along
the edges, feels tiny stones, straps, laces.
Hopes he won't have to pee.

He listens, but can't hear any sound now
except a wailing siren from the street.
Is Mama dead? He wants to pound the door
and scream but knows the stinging buckle.
He nuzzles Mama's dresses, smells her smell,
then twists a piece of hem until he falls asleep.

Waking stiff and cold, he's bewildered
for a moment, then grabs the knob
and bursts into the morning light.
Mama's snoring in their bed.
He dares not wake her. Sour milk
for cereal, no one to tie his sneakers.
He'll watch cartoons on the snowflake TV.
Mama will sleep til noon.

Lyla, 1992

I stop to have a cup of tea with Lyla.
Nearly eighty, she counsels parents of suicides,
shows me a photo of a pony-tailed teen.

My daughter slashed her wrists, she says.
She says her husband, now deceased,
used to cater fancy meals for Broadway stars.

OJ was there once, she says, grinning.
*He was something. He could park his shoes
under my bed anytime.*

Ballerina

She's eleven or twelve, twigs and knobs,
sitting at the table with friends – pink
leotards, hair netted and pinned into buns.

They dig into plates brimming with salad.
She, pale as snow, cuts her burger
into bite-size pieces.

Arm arced, she says, *Watch me.* Forefinger
and thumb drop a morsel toward her open
mouth, and miss. The girls giggle. Nothing

passes her lips. What remains on her plate
she submerges in a water glass,
sprinkles salt and pepper.

Child, it hurts to watch you.
Who will catch you when you stumble?

As if on silent cue, the girls grab up backpacks,
jostle, disappear, scraps of high-pitched
chatter linger.

Maria
Curacao, 1957

On Roberto's lantern-lit patio,
we listened to Latino music,
played card games,
ate tapas for the first time.
His sister, Maria, not yet sixteen,
lapis-colored eyes, dark curls,
her cheeks uncommonly bright.
Perhaps she knew (we couldn't say)
this would be her last Christmas.

By day, we gathered, drinking
Dutch chocolate from porcelain cups,
while overhead fans shifted
sultry tropical air. Outside
the lilt of papiemento mingled
with the scent of hibiscus.
We swam in the surf, spent
moonlit evenings dancing too close.

Glistening cruise ships crowded
the tiny harbor, tourists swayed
on the pontoon bridge.
Sun-washed, stepped houses.
Cobblestone marketplace:
tomatoes, guavas, spices,
sugar cane, plantains,
burlap bags filled with coffee beans
hawked among the swirl of
flowered cotton and bare feet.

William

William comes to my office asking for help.
Despite the clean shirt and jeans, he looks as if
he's just escaped from the bone wagon.

Are you on the cocktail? I ask.
No, he says, *when I take it with methadone I get really sick.*

*

William drives me to check out his new apartment
in a new Saturn, borrowed, I hope.
He's extremely polite, soft-spoken. I'm beginning
to like him more than I should.
He pulls up to a gas station, gets out, and tells
the attendant to fill it with Super.

Then he pops his head into the car and says:

> *When I was eight, my mother left me on a street*
> *corner, told me to wait. She never came back.*
> *I hung around until a black lady took me home*
> *and raised me with her own. Skinny Latino kid*
> *in the projects, I got beat up every day.*

This is more than I need to know. The deal's been struck.

Back on the road, he says:

> *To stay alive, I sold drugs, heroin mostly. I was good*
> *at it, made lots of money, didn't use. Curiosity finally*
> *fucked me up. With my T-cell count, I should be dead.*

We've breached the line, so I ask, *Are they okay?*

continued...

They're both free, he says. *Jessica wanted a baby. It's a miracle, don't you think?*

I don't say what I think: Get off the damn methadone, get on meds.
You made a son, now be a father.

*

The apartment's in a clean building. We move from room to room.
I test light switches, flush toilet, turn on hot water.
William trails me, a hapless lamb, *thank you, thank you.*
No swagger, not the brash dealer who did a stretch.

I find an excuse to call him every month.

His wife runs off with another man, gives him the child.
He can't get off the methadone, buys his son a puppy

Sends me a photo of William, Jr., on his second birthday,
chubby, wide-eyed, and smiling.

The Patriarch's Wall

In late afternoon, blinds drawn,
Jorge sits stiffly on the sofa,
corded hands immobile on his lap.

He strains to hear Teresa's laughter,
hears only the child's high-pitched call.
On the wall, votive light plays

across a silver crucifix, a rosary,
a painted triptych
gilded by his mother's hand.

Sometimes he misses work, thirty years
of laying dead to ground. Hard, dark earth
taking back its own. Each night he scrubbed clean

his muddy boots, countering Death
with every stroke. Now a weak heart
makes him trouble when he rises from his bed.

Slammed door, Teresa's youngest scrambles
onto his lap, unfolds a crumpled drawing.
He strokes her hair, squints at the scribbled lines.

Please, Poppi, put it on the wall near Jesus.
The child tugs on his knotty hand.
He struggles to his feet, wants to please her.

Come, we'll hang it in a sunny place.

Part III
Across Time

Sweet Fourteen
USO, Miami Beach, 1952

My cousin Mickey stuffs my bra, paints
my nails Ruby Red. Spritzing me with Shalimar,

she clucks with sixteen-year-old super cool,
Try not to giggle.

Inside the smoky auditorium, half the fleet
is dancing cheek-to-cheek with girls in flirty

flowered dresses. *Be careful,* Mickey warns,
someone always spikes the punch bowl.

She tosses her blonde hair, quickly lands a sailor,
blows me a kiss, leaving me against the wall.

A southern drawl, *Come here often?*
My heart skips, he's gorgeous. *I'm Kenny.*

He draws my arms around his neck, presses
my back until I feel the rhythm of his hips.

To his questions, I mumble *No* or *Yes.*
I'm not a confident liar yet.

While the jukebox croons *Heart and Soul,*
Kenny whispers, *I like shy girls.*

A new sailor's arm around her waist, Mickey
winks at me. *Let's go get Wolfie's hot pastrami.*

Later, parked along the jetty, Mickey's cracking
jokes, smoking Luckies. I'm in the back seat

continued...

getting a crash course in French-kissing.
From the USS Seacat, Kenny sends another

steamy letter. *We're heading out,* he writes.
I miss you already. He never asked how old I was.

Passing Through Northern New Jersey
in Late August, 1959

    for Hank

We drove your rusty Ford pickup from Gregory, Michigan
to Upper Montclair; two gypsies, tired and hot. We argued

the last hundred miles. Their mock Tudor home teeming
with newspapers, magazines, books. Five unstrung rackets.

A toboggan propped against the living room mantel.
Your mom wiped her hands on her apron, hugged you,

and fidgeted. Did we realize we'd come a day early?
The guestroom hadn't been tidied up for me yet.

At dinner, she scurried about with platters, finding
any excuse to touch your shoulder, your arm. Your dad,

a retired economist, asked, *Why mathematics?* as if
you'd never had this conversation before, as if you hadn't

been home in years. You, a heartbeat away from a Ph.D., said,
Tomorrow I'll mow the lawn for you, while I busied myself

navigating the bloody capon and wilted salad. Coffee
was served in the living room, knee-to-knee. Furniture pushed

to the center to make space for cartons labeled Christmas
tree lights, bric-a-brac, Meg's things. Conversation about folks

I didn't know. Later, I overheard you and your dad quarreling.
The next morning we left for Manhattan.

continued...

By the time you figured out you wanted more than
a summer fling, I'd gone back to Chicago, found a new boyfriend.

Now I sit among my dusty cartons, and remember how
keen I was back then on discarding, traveling light. I never told you

I got a card from your mom. I'd left a white hankie; she'd washed
and ironed it, neatly folded it into the envelope, with a note saying,

It was so nice to meet you. I hope you can come again soon.

Paradise Italian Style

We got lost south of Bologna, driving through
strange hills, rain pounding on the car

like a furious *strega*. At eleven p.m., no road signs,
just kilometers of slippery road going

nowhere. Suddenly the wipers caught a lighted
sign atop a ridge – *Avanti! Piccolo Paradiso.*

"*Mi dispiace*, the hotel isn't open," the desk clerk
greeted us, two drenched Americans dispossessed.

Undaunted, you pointed to the noisy dining room.
"Ah, special party but *la cucina* she is closed."

That's when I lost resolve and cried.

At the table, six sloshed men, beet-faced
and wheezing, their women frowsy, except

a blonde, draped on two barrel-chested men,
belting out a stream of raunchy songs.

Two sullen waiters stared at their watches.
We passed on eel, chose ravioli and regional Lambrusco,

a fizzy wine with too much tickle. Bought a case
for the promise of a cabin with fresh linen.

Across the muddy paddock, a row of narrow cabins,
lone floodlight like a crooked finger beckoned.

continued...

Hefting soggy bags and a bottle of Lambrusco,
we reached the door on planks laid end-to-end.

Inside, we dislodged a furry poacher, sent a rage
of shadows scurrying up the dampish walls.

The sign above the sink read *Non Potabile*.
The roof leaked in staccato.

We settled on the lumpy bed, uncorked
the wine, convinced we'd been lured to Hell.

Faculty Wives, Circa 1968

Behind Edwards Place rowhouses, we courted
security with home-grown tomatoes,
while marijuana thrived in the corn stalks.

We harvested it in Lindy's bathtub, got high
listening to Fleetwood Mac.
Past midnight we drove up Nassau Street.

Headlights' glare – naked men, penises flopping,
white asses suspended like Santa's reindeer.
In a flash, they disappeared down Witherspoon Street.

We shook our heads. It's the weed.

We fixed leaky faucets, drummed ABCs
while we scooped in strained carrots, safety-pinned
socks before we dropped them in bleach.

How we adored Melvin as he strode around
campus like a French musketeer, green velvet cloak
flaring, plumed hat cocked at a naughty angle.

In a rented farmhouse, students' toothbrushes
lined up, electricity sporadic, Melvin taught
Religion 203 from index cards, shuffled.

We joined in a circle on the rough wood floor,
candles flickering; passed around joints
until even the flies seemed disoriented.

We sipped afternoon tea with the deans' wives,
tie-dyed our T-shirts, tucked our toddlers
in strollers and marched in the protests.

continued...

Then there was Maggie with curly red hair
and freckles. She smuggled hashish from Tunis,
smiling right past customs with two drooling

babies, diaper bag never suspected,
while agents ripped our luggage apart, squeezed
toothpaste all over our lingerie.

We clucked over freshmen, cultured our yogurt,
slipped into satin and danced a mean fox trot
with department chairmen.

We were fearless. Of course, we inhaled.
How else could we float in the moment?

Snapshot of an Ivy League Faculty Wife

This Saturday morning
I'm sitting cross-legged on the bare wood
floor of the Chancellor Green rotunda,
my long hair pulled back and wearing
my husband's Oxford shirt, sleeves rolled up,
wide-band mod watch – it's the late sixties.

Tonight's the faculty Christmas dance.
My assignment – whip up a diamond-stud
décor, lots of pizzazz and greenery.
Would garlands of balsam
look more festive wound around
columns or swagged from balcony railings?

Later, I slip into a chocolate velvet gown,
darken my brows, dab on pale lipstick.
Oh so late to the dance, eight of us
stoned, laughing at nothing and everything,
until someone gets wildly silly, sets fire
to the linen tablecloth.

My husband's chairman asks me to dance,
his arm brushing my breast, his fingers
weaving through my dark hair.
The sacrificial lamb, I keep smiling,
oh how I keep smiling, and the band
won't stop playing fox-trots.

Counting Backwards in London

On this fine Sunday afternoon, I was alone
in the flat when George and his two mates
arrived, and George, having had too many pints
at the pub down the road, wanted to stay,
but his mates kept insisting they had to leave,
they'd be late returning to base, then George,
a captain in the British Army, was careening
down our long hall on my three-year-old son's
tricycle, bent on counting backwards to the last
time we'd seen each other, on a Salisbury
golf course, George on his belly on the grass
showing me how to take the lie of each hole
for its strategic location, much the same way
he'd taken aim at smugglers' camels crossing
the mountains in Yemen or when he'd combed
Belfast for booby traps and homemade bombs,
and I wanted him to stay longer, wanted him
sober, so we could relive the races, games
of pontoon, darts, high tea in his mum's garden,
because, as his mates dragged him off
the tricycle and managed to stand him upright,
we had no idea if we'd ever see each other
again and I'll always remember his broad smile
and how his blond hair flopped across
his forehead when he turned at the top
of the stairs and said, *I'll come to America
next spring to see you,* and he did.

Life Cycle of Argument

At first, we argued constantly. We were loud
and unruly. The spindle chair was my favorite
weapon; he preferred bone china.
Sometimes we resorted to flinging ashtrays.
Smoking was still in fashion.

Arguments evolved: whose turn to sort
the recyclables escalated to who belongs
to the black thong I found in your pocket?
Four hundred dollar shoes?
You said you were going to Kmart.

We cursed a lot: bitch/bastard/upyours
punctuated every sentence. It was liberating.
Arguments always ended in the bedroom.
Beet-faced and sweaty, we flopped onto
the goose-down. Sex was lusty. Life good.

Our voices turned reedy, our house in tatters.
We slept in separate bedrooms, argued about
how to quit arguing, numbered arguments
from one to a hundred, memorized the list.
We talked about the past, stirred the ashes.

Silence. Neighbors thanked us. We posted
numbers on the microwave: my favorite, #3,
you never loved me; his, #16, you never listen.
We had time to exercise, grow vegetables,
read, line our pockets with stones.

Across Time

He returns to his office after class, finds her
wedged between two policemen.
She pulls away, throws herself into his arms.
She's trashed her husband's office across the hall,
bit him on the nose, sending him
to the emergency room for stitches.
The policemen aren't sure what to do.
I'll see that she leaves the building, he assures them.

She sits in his leather office chair, sobbing,
I can't believe there's nothing else left.
He says, *You've been estranged a long time.*
He kisses her on the cheek and walks her outside.

That evening, they go to a restaurant. *I come here a lot,*
she says, tracing the lines on the checkered tablecloth.
*A good part of my life has been discussed and negotiated
over these tables. I've been scolded, seduced, bored,
sometimes even amused.*

He leans forward in the chair, rests his arms on the table.
*You have to control your anger. It's not going to get you
anywhere.*
You're right, she says, knows this is what he wants to hear.
What's going to happen, she presses him, *when it's over?*
You'll learn to endure, he says.
She shakes her dark hair, as if to say, that's not enough.

They order a meal. *You've known me for years,* she says.
What do you think of me? She knows the doors
he will never open.

Her smile takes him off-guard. How do I deal with this woman?
I think you're interesting, he says, which is not at all what
he meant to say, *and...I think you're trouble.*

*

She's invited to his retirement party, but decides not to go.
Tries on different excuses, but, in the end, just doesn't
show up.

They meet for lunch. She stares at his hands, the noticeable
tremor. *It's benign*, he says.

He's in a rush. One of his former students has arranged
a TV interview; he doesn't want to be late.
She says, *We could have done this another time.*
I have plenty of time, he says, glancing at his watch.

The fire of her anger, what was most destructive,
had bound him to her. She has learned proportion.

They grope for conversation. She tells him her last
boarder went home to Capetown. She's taken in another
– a young Israeli who's lecturing at the University.

He says he's gotten a pacemaker. *If I'm lucky,*
I get a pretty girl to pat me down when I by-pass
airport security. He checks his watch again,
then signals for the bill.

Across time, she has learned to conjure him
as younger, more vigorous. His mind faster
than blue lightning. That intensity now
fixed on extracting a credit card from his wallet.

Negotiating

Hamid and I are sitting on a stack of rugs
in one of those *going out of business* Oriental rug
stores along Route 1, negotiating over two small
prayer rugs that I sort of like, but could live without,
except that I'm in the mood to buy something,
and usually when I'm feeling that way, I gravitate
toward tribal rugs, rolling them back, one by one,
stroking their pile, tracing stylized flowers and animals,
heat rising from deep reds and blues, then Hamid
gets up and heads to his office, returns with a pitcher
of cold tea, some dates, and an orange, which he deftly
peels, while he tells me he's planning to close the store
soon, he has heart trouble, and no customers, even with
the huge banner flapping out front, and if this is true,
I figure it's a good time to bargain if you can call it
a bargain when women spend lifetimes bent over looms,
fingers cracked and discolored from tedious dyeing,
combing, spinning, weaving, and clipping, only income
besides raising a few chickens and goats, while
their men bundle rugs and cart them to markets, sell
them for a fraction of what I'm willing to pay,
and I ask Hamid what he will do with his inventory,
and he says his cousin in Camden will take the rugs,
it's for the best, each day is precious, and in a few
weeks I'll drop in to see Hamid again, we'll have
the same conversation, but those rugs will be cheaper.

The Clock Repairer

Fingers too blunt to clean and assemble
delicate clock parts: gears, coils, screws,
painted faces, pendulums, chimes.
The English had an orderly clockmakers' trade,
he says. *Not the French – a free-for-all.*

He caresses the hip-like panel of a tall case clock.
French country, he says, muscular arm disappearing
up the rolled sleeve of a taut T-shirt.

Have you always repaired clocks?
No, ma'am. State trooper, twenty-five years.

Explain this: I was pulled over by a trooper.
You were going 75 mph, he says.
I say, I've got cruise control.
Seat belt citation is cheaper, your choice, ma'am.

Activity reports, the clock repairer says. *It's about
not coming in with a blank sheet. Never
arrested a nun, but drunk clergy are fair game.*

What about racial profiling?
*Sure we did. Who's more likely to carry a gun?
We could get blown away like that.* Snaps fingers.
Can you blame us?

I have a wall clock, I say, that doesn't run.
French or English? he asks.
Swedish, it's got an ornate gilt case, pendulum,
heirloom...

The clock repairer lounges against a display case,
liquid eyes tick, tick. I'm his only customer.
Bring your clock in, he says. *I'll be happy to fix it.*

At The Alchemist & Barrister
Princeton, New Jersey

It could have been decades earlier, closer to
the marches and water hoses. We'd entered the pub
of a popular restaurant, our reflections caught
in the mirror above the bar. White male heads
snapped in our direction. In the split second it would
take a strobe to fracture motion, a blue charge tore
through the room. I felt your body tense. Ready.
You stepped closer, put your hand on my shoulder.
Talk stopped. Only smoke curls and the running
mouth of a TV announcer. *Let's leave*, I said,
but I knew you'd never back down.
Then, by some silent cue, the drinkers' hustle
started up again. The hostess asked if we wanted
to be seated in the pub or the main dining room.
Here, I said, staring down a beefy blond guy
who didn't avert his eyes, piquing him to imagine
a white woman and a fine, dark-skinned man
as lovers, while the basketball game splashed across
the screen. Later, a raucous cheer, as if
every male wished he'd been the black man
who'd sunk that long three-pointer at the buzzer.

Dialogue in Black and White

My hand breaks the fall, flips me
onto grass, head missing cement,
nothing broken, heel of my hand
bloody, throbbing.

Security cop, dark, long-boned,
weapon holstered, reaches out, grips
my arm. Inside the cafeteria, I say,
too shaken to drive, *Please stay.*

I'm here as long as you need me,
he says, thick-knuckled fingers, agile
as a wide-receiver's, plastic-
wrapping ice cubes.

Corded veins branch up his arms.
Did you play football? I ask.
Years ago, he says, *now I coach
in PAL. Kids need role models,
discipline.*

I say, *I have two sons – one white,
one black. It's as if I'm two mothers.
I never know how…*

He scans my face, leans across
the table, open palm, fingers splayed
in space. *Out think them,* he says,
You're smarter than they are.

I want to enter his dense skin, crisp
uniform, his hands which pluck
the spiraling ball from the air.

Hampstead Again

for Billy and Jimmy

On a snowy day, when the neighborhood
has gone quiet, except for the plows,
I'm peeling onions, stripping layers of fat
from a pot roast, sizzling oil in the pan.

And it's Hampstead again. Grey leaden
skies, damp warning its way through
our clothes. Along the streets where Keats
took a turn, past the chemist, the ironmonger,
I'm choosing grapes, lettuce, fresh beets,
and tomatoes at the greengrocer's.
You two are juggling oranges and apples.
At the butcher's, you kick up sawdust,
giggle at pigs' feet, fake gag at the tongue
and the tripe until a stern Brit scolds you both.
Short hop to the bakery where a plump-faced
clerk greets us: *Right wet one we're havin'.*
I pay for warm yeasty loaves; you wolf down
jam tarts as if you haven't eaten in days.
Then the ten-block walk home loaded
with parcels. I sidestep puddles; you splash
about like irreverent ducks.

While the roast simmers, I curl up
with a book, any one will do, and listen for
echoes of the lively dinners,
when we gathered at table, forks ready.

Noodle Doctor

I visited a Chinese noodle doctor.

She examined me with chopsticks

and declared my edible parts overcooked.

Is there a cure?

She shook her head.

Can't you do anything?

She ripped open her starched white coat,

a rooster tattooed on her breast.

She stretched her neck to crow,

tangled with the hanging plants,

and nearly choked to death.

Teterboro Airport

for Philip (1937-2007)

I'd waited more than fifteen years for the phone call,
which came from Teterboro Airport.
You always knew you'd be a pilot. For forty years, you
crossed continents, delivered cargo, ferried
single engine props, corporate jets. I was terrified to fly.

That day at Teterboro, a layover while winding up
the sale. *Just called to say hello,* you said. *How are you?*
I'm fine, I said, *and you?* The unasked question
circled like a 747 with jammed landing gear.
Finally, *I'll be back next month,* you said. *Can I see you?*

We met in the city, a Broadway show, late supper,
a suite at the St. Regis, where we squabbled over
my mother. You defended her, chastised me;
I said, *Forget it, she's dead.* In that moment, we knew
whatever might have happened, never would.

A few years later, I saw you for the last time. Battling
tremors, you refused to let me drive. Locked your elbows,
grasped the steering wheel, and said, *Relax.* I assured
myself you knew your limits. We had lunch. Laughed
about the night that grounded us for good.

Antigua

It wasn't always like this, the driver says, pointing
        to wrecked stone windmills, blades rotted off.
On casual paved roads, we pass tin-roofed out-
        houses, scraggly palms, bailing wire.

Used to be lots of sugar cane. Gone. Rains
        no longer come this way.
Old tires stacked on sides of ditches, black goats,
        ears tagged, nibbling scrub.

Dusty schoolyard, children in blue uniforms
        jumping rope, chasing. Near a banyan tree,
hexagonal yellow sign: NO DRUGS. NO GUNS.
        Things are different now, the driver says.

From a bluff, clear aquamarine stretches to the horizon.
        We stop for frosty mai tais at a gated
resort and yacht club. The driver pockets a tip
        from a guard in starched whites.

Returning to Saint Johns, its pastel houses, bustling
        market, bright cottons, beads, grizzled
men with dreads beating on steel drums,
        Next time you stay longer, the driver says.

Along the quay, Colombian Emeralds, Rolex, Gucci,
        glistening ships off-load tourists.
The driver shakes his head. *My children want to leave.*
        Nothing to keep us here, they say.

Red Skelton on the Ponte Vecchio

Dusk. A red-haired man with a rubbery face browses
gold in a brightly-lit stall. I'm shoulder to shoulder
with Clem Kadiddlehopper, my Tuesday night regular,
his left arm circling the waist of a six-foot blonde.
My brain's ablaze. I try on words: *Willy Lump-Lump.
San Fernando Red. Laugh, can't stop.* I open my mouth,
but like Freddy the Freeloader, nothing comes out.
As if he'd read my mind, Red tips his cap, then blasts a smile.
His angel pouts, and they disappear in the milling crowd.

Revelation

It's hard to forget Gary, hips loose-jointed
between passion and tomorrow. Knock at
my door, that cocky grin, wanting to talk,
stay the night. *Do you know why Gary doesn't
answer my calls?* I ask, sipping espresso.

I really couldn't say. Paul's eyes fix
on a spot over my left shoulder. A silken wedge,
sun-bleached to bone, flops over his right brow.
I want to reach across the varnished wood, weave
my fingers through it. Instead I circle a spoon
in my cup. Check my lipstick in an oval pocket
mirror. Check my watch. It's still ticking.

Clamor in the bar ratchets up my fear.
Do you think Gary's involved with someone else?
Paul leans forward, blue lucid eyes demanding:
Are you sure you want the answer? No mistake.
I'm face-to-face with Gary's lover.

Saturday Night Alone, I Surf the Net

searching for the men who got away.
Lost one to Duke by way of Jakarta, another
retired from the math department at Ohio State.
A young blond lover, without compass, set sail
for Arizona; others knew what they wanted:
educator, rabbi, pilot. The pilot ferried planes
all over the world; I was eager to nest.
I download live speeches by an aging radical
who still trumpets the cause of racial injustice.
Discover a memoir penned by a doctor
who'd cared for third-world kids. Some fought
over me, like the fine-looking Greek on his way
to becoming a famed biblical scholar.
He'd been a Golden Gloves champ, his hands
lethal weapons, which held off smashing the jaw
of my ex-boyfriend-stalker, now the Maestro
of a vocal school in Toronto. I google my ex,
great reviews of his books on blind men
and English cathedrals. Where are my kudos
for surviving twenty-three years of marriage?
Here is my dentist, a battle-scarred biker,
decades since we've been intimate
about anything except my teeth.
First love, born on the Fourth of July,
trapped in the Social Security Death Index.

Safe Place at Wilder Park

for Peter (1937-1983)

It's always like this.
You lean against
the trunk, slouch
slightly, smile.
Blond hair flops across
your brow.
We were both eleven
when we climbed the tree,
straddled limbs,
and traded secrets.
We didn't care
the tree belonged to him,
until the day
he appeared, shotgun
at his side.

Now I'm fleeing
toward you.
My dark skirt flecked
with violets
whips about my legs.
I'm out of breath.
I lean into your arms.
My heart skips
a beat, then calms.

About the Author

Nancy Scott's first full-length book of poetry, *Down to the Quick*, was published by Plain View Press in 2007. She is the current managing editor of *U.S.1 Worksheets*, the journal of the U.S.1 Poets' Cooperative in New Jersey. Nancy has spent decades advocating for homeless families, foster children, and the mentally ill. She is the adoptive parent of three interracial children. Many of her poems evolved from stories she heard in her work. She has been awarded a residency at Ragdale and nominated three times for the Pushcart Prize.

Nancy Scott
Lawrenceville, New Jersey
609-637-9736
nscott29@aol.com
http://www.nancyscott.net

Princeton, 1968

About the Artist

Robert V.P. Davis studied at the Maryland Institute College of Art and earned a Diploma in Fine Arts Painting. Mr. Davis' work as a painter, sculptor, designer and illustrator has been exhibited in Maryland, New York, Washington D.C., Virginia, Pennsylvania, Chicago, Utah and Los Angeles, as well as in Sinop and Ankara, Turkey. He has received numerous awards over the years.

Robert says, "These trees are an expression of my appreciation for and concern about the destruction of the world's forests and woodlands."

Robert V. P. Davis
Baltimore, Maryland
410-235-9099
artist@theartistathand.com
http:// theartistathand.com